Time Management

Increasing Your Time Utilization: Effective Methods For Enhancing Productivity

(Revealing The Proven Techniques For Efficient Time Management)

Norman Lockwood

TABLE OF CONTENT

Chapter 1: Setting Smart Goals 1

Chapter 2: Spend Less Time On Less Vital Responsibilities. 6

Chapter 3: The Easy Method That Transformed Me From Average To Superstar 13

Chapter 4: How To Safeguard Your Most Valuable Possession 18

Chapter 5: How To Schedule A Perfect Week Ahead 28

Chapter 6: Time Management Strategies For Achieving Your Objectives 33

Chapter 7: Common Time Blocking Errors And Ways To Prevent Them 42

Chapter 8: Tips For Creating A Productive To-Do List 50

Chapter 9: Some Suggestions To Reduce Distractions And Improve Concentration 64

Chapter 10: Proceed Wherever Your Energy Leads You. 70

Chapter 11: Declutter Your Days 82

Chapter 12: Effective Time Routines 106

Chapter 13: Consider Your Time And Energy Resources 112

Chapter 14: Utilize An Effective To-Do List 119

Conclusion 125

Chapter 1: Setting Smart Goals

Setting objectives is essential for effective time management strategies. It is the single most important life skill that the vast majority of people never properly acquire. Goal-setting is applicable to every aspect of your life, including your finances, health, personal growth, relationships, and even your spirituality. According to Brian Tracy's book objectives, less than 3 percent of people have written, specific objectives and a strategy for achieving them. Establishing objectives places you ahead of the pack!

Some individuals attribute every misfortune in their lives to something or someone else. They assume the victim role and surrender all of their power and control. Successful individuals instead commit themselves to assuming responsibility for their lives, regardless of unforeseeable or uncontrollable occurrences. The past cannot be changed, and the future is a direct consequence of your actions in the present moment!

Les trois P's

Setting significant, long-term objectives is a significant step toward achieving one's aspirations. In turn, setting and achieving short-term objectives can help you complete the duties required to reach long-term objectives. It is also essential to ensure that all of your objectives harness the power of the three Ps:

POSITIVE: Who could be motivated by the objective, "Find a career that is not dull?" Goals should be stated in a positive manner so that you feel good about yourself and what you're attempting to achieve. A better alternative could be: "Enroll in pre-law courses so I can one day assist people with legal issues."

PERSONAL: Goals must be individual. Not those of friends, family, or the media. Always include the pronoun "I" in your objective statement to make it yours. When your objectives are personal, you will be more motivated to succeed and more satisfied with your achievements.

POSSIBLE: Consider what is feasible and within your control when establishing objectives. Admission to an Ivy League university may be possible if you are performing well academically, but it is unlikely if you are underperforming. In the latter instance, a more reasonable objective may be to enroll in a college or vocational school that offers courses related to your desired profession. You could also engage in volunteer labor to enhance your college applications.

The SMART Method

SMART is a convenient acronym for the set of criteria that a goal must possess for the goal achiever to realize it.

In his book The Success Principles, success coach Jack Canfield writes, "Vague goals produce vague results." To achieve an objective, you must have a precise understanding of what you want.

Creating a list of the benefits that achieving your objective will bring to your life provides your mind with a compelling reason to pursue it.

You must be able to track your progress towards your objective in order to achieve it. For this reason, all goals require a form of objective measurement so that you can remain on track and be motivated by the sweet taste of quantifiable progress.

Achievable: Setting ambitious objectives is commendable, but setting unrealistic objectives will demotivate you. A good objective is one that is challenging, but not so unrealistic that it is virtually impossible to achieve.

Relevant: Prior to setting goals, it's a good idea to define your fundamental values and life purpose, as these are the factors that will ultimately determine how and what goals you choose. In and of themselves, goals do not produce pleasure. Goals that align with our life's mission have the ability to make us joyful.

Without a deadline, there is no compelling reason or motivation to begin working towards your objectives. By establishing a deadline, your subconscious mind begins working night and day to bring you closer to achieving your objective.

Chapter 2: Spend Less Time On Less Vital Responsibilities.

Cooking requires considerable effort. When you have a child, it is essential to keep the kitchen and morning routines simple. It works if you make tasks like sorting laundry or cleaning up a mess enjoyable for him or her. Make an effort to make his responsibilities more pleasurable. Do not be afraid to seek for help. You will need to barter with your mother so that she will keep your child for a day so that you can attend to some urgent matters.

Introduce your infant to the concept of doing chores. If your child does not see the value in tidying up after him or herself, you may need to compensate him or her. Your child will become more accustomed to assisting you.

I am responsible for preparing dinner. I prepare two dishes per day. These are my morning and midday meals. There are many children who do not have to cook when their mother is present. They always have access to quick food restaurants. My offspring are an exception. Dinnertime is family time.

The amount of time you spend in the kitchen will increase. As children mature into adolescents, they seek greater independence in the household.

Try to limit your weekly shopping excursions to just one. Take the opportunity to go shopping once per week. It will reduce the amount of time and money you spend on dining.

Create a household budget. Do not depend on credit.

A family budget will save you a great deal of time and money. You can choose what to spend money on, what not to spend money on, and how much of each category of spending to restrict. You can also create a family credit card budget.

Reduce spending on your offspring

Children always want more toys, diversions, and other items that can be purchased with money. If you give them everything they want, you will spend more money on them. You should not overindulge. If you do not give them everything they desire, they will refuse to share their possessions with you.

Offer your children a choice. Don't coerce them into doing what you want. If they don't want to do what you want, don't force them to.

Always seek inexpensive alternatives to fast cuisine. There are some less expensive options, such as using a restaurant coupon. However, when it comes to fast food, some parents may overindulge their children by purchasing expensive food for them. Instead of purchasing costly fast food for your children, take the time to plan ahead. Create a list of food alternatives that are affordable and of higher quality.

4) Regularly Review Your Calendar

Reviewing your calendar is an excellent method to organize your day and prioritize tasks. It also maintains you aware of your obligations, allowing you to prepare for unforeseen events. Reviewing your calendar daily, or at the very least once per week, guarantees that nothing falls through the gaps. This is particularly essential if you are juggling multiple projects or have a full work schedule.

By routinely reviewing your calendar, you can ensure that everything is completed on time and on schedule. And by putting your most essential tasks first, you will be able to immediately begin working on them. For example, your agenda may include a client meeting at 8:00 a.m. and a staff meeting at 9:00 a.m. If you check your schedule before leaving for work, you'll see that even though they're back-to-back, they're separated by hours, and it's likely that you'll be able to complete both duties without feeling rushed or stressed.

However, if you don't take a moment to review your calendar when you wake up in the morning, you may wind up being late for your appointments because you assumed they were close together.

Today's To-Do List: We all have tasks we wish to accomplish but never seem to have the time. The today's tasks schedule is one method for staying organized and managing unplanned activities throughout the day. Even during meetings, keep a notepad nearby and jot down any new ideas as soon as they occur to you. Then, whenever possible, cram these tasks into any small windows of leisure time that may exist throughout the day.

These small moments will rapidly add up if utilized effectively! Suppose, for instance, you have an hour-long lunch break at work. If you plan ahead by writing three or four tasks on your to-do list for today, you will be able to complete them as soon as you return from lunch instead of waiting until the evening when it is too late to get anything done. It is also essential that these tasks can be completed quickly; there is no need to overburden yourself with long-term projects or lengthy reports when there are other matters that require your immediate attention. And if you ever feel overwhelmed by too many tasks at once, take a moment to prioritize the tasks on your schedule before returning to the task you were working on before.

This way, you won't feel as if everything needs to be completed immediately, which helps you maintain composure while completing your daily tasks.

There are numerous methods to ensure that nothing falls through the cracks. One popular method is to create a list of tasks to be completed the following day before heading to bed each night. This enables you to wake up knowing exactly where you stand and to begin each day without having to worry about forgetting anything essential. However, some individuals prefer using calendars rather than lists because calendars provide them with greater flexibility in scheduling their days according to their priorities, as opposed to simply listing everything in chronological order from beginning to end.

Chapter 3: The Easy Method That Transformed Me From Average To Superstar

On Day 4, there is no doubt that your usefulness increased dramatically. If you did not, then you must return and ensure that you are focusing on your list and following the given rules.

If you are anything like me, then I'm willing to wager that you had difficulty initiating your largest A-level assignment. This task was likely the most important thing you could have completed that day and contributed the most to achieving your objectives. Because this is a problem that everyone confronts, you can breathe easy. I refer to this mission as your "Winged serpent" and today you will find out how to kill it.

Once Upon A Time Throughout history, there are numerous accounts of saints embarking on perilous journeys. In a large number of these tales, princesses, towns, or kingdoms are saved by slaying mythical creatures. When the hero emerges victorious at the conclusion of each of these tales, he receives an enormous reward. This prize could be gold, popularity, or the same enchanting damsel.

Here are some exceptional details for you. Those equivalent rewards can be yours. You can become the legend of your own story if you begin each day by slaying your dragon.

Learning this procedure and cultivating the habit of doing it consistently will propel you from the top 10% to the top 1% of the world's most valuable people. When you conceal this tendency, you will become a relentless force of efficiency. The trap?

It is also likely the most difficult undertaking to accomplish.

Slaying Your Dragon

How then would we slay our legendary beast? Let's begin by defining a mythical creature.

Simply stated, your winged serpent is the most important task of the day. This is the task that will have the greatest impact on your life and career. This is also typically the most difficult task for you to complete and will require the most effort to get everything moving. On the other hand, completing this task will provide you with the maximum amount of endorphins and will fuel you for the remainder of the day. Consider it productivity's Viagra.

The majority of people begin their day by completing quick and basic tasks that require little effort. They typically justify to themselves that they are accounting for their extensive afternoon activities. How frequently do they eventually reach it? Perhaps 20% of the time.

This style of thinking is referred to as sluggishness, and we are largely responsible for it.

According to our friend Pareto, these errands only enhance your day. I like to think of it this way: If you knew you had to fight a mythical serpent today and you knew you could defeat it, but it would be difficult, would you spend the entire day lounging? Would you spend your day reading messages, returning phone calls, and attending social events, or would you simply get it over with as quickly as possible?

If you select the first option, I can guarantee that during the time you wait, you will magnify the difficulty in your mind and make it seem more daunting than it actually is. While avoiding their mythical serpents, the overwhelming majority will end up doing one of three things:

- Save it for the end, when they can't devote as much concentration and energy to it, so that it will take longer to complete and be of inferior quality.

- Bring it home from work or stay conscious until late at night while detesting the same work that will bring them closer to their goals (no one brings low-value work home).

- Postpone it until the following day, and then the following day, and then the following day...

Imagine how amazing you would feel after slaying a legendary serpent. You experience the dopamine-filled pleasure of vanity because, where it matters, you realize that you have accomplished something extraordinary. Is there a compelling reason why you wouldn't want to feel this way in the morning? The longer you stand by, the less time you need to develop an extraordinary perspective of yourself.

Chapter 4: How To Safeguard Your Most Valuable Possession

Therefore, if you are tired of wasting your valuable time, you must protect it at all costs. That might appear excessive. But I am sincere. As stated by Jim Rohn, "either you run the day, or the day runs you."

Learn to organize your time effectively. The only way you will be able to preserve your time is to first determine how you will employ it precisely. Obviously, this will differ from person to person. And it could change over time.

For example, in your twenties, your primary objective may have been to start your own business. After starting a family, however, things changed. Despite the fact that your company remains a major priority in your life, your family has taken the top spot.

Then, where do you start? If you want to achieve optimal time management, you must set goals and adhere to them. "Goals are like a map,". They provide us with a starting point and detailed instructions on how to reach our destination. They also help us maintain concentration. If you've ever traveled in a foreign country, you know how important it is to keep your eyes on the road so you don't overlook a turn.

In addition to setting goals, you can also attempt the following college strategies:
Create an exhaustive inventory.
Utilize a matrix of priorities to determine what to do, delegate, delete, or discontinue.
Concentrate solely on your MITs; these are the three most important duties of the day.
Observe the 80/20 Rule.
Start with what you detest.
Be mindful of dates and due dates.

Keep a journal of your work for reference purposes.

Ask yourself, like another Philadelphia icon, Benjamin Franklin, "What good should I do today?"

After determining your priorities, you can then determine how you would like to devote your time.

Capture "time thieves."

I wish I had invented this term. But, it's regrettable. It was the singular Kevin Kruse.

According to Kevin, examples of "time thieves" include the following:

Meetings. They typically begin late, are poorly managed, and conclude with no tangible results. It is not surprising that Mark Cuban is not a devotee, as he is of his Dallas Mavericks. Only schedule a meeting if it serves a purpose, or as the Cubans would say, if someone is giving you a check.

Email. According to Kruse's research, this is the "number one factor hindering their productivity." Because they are a constant distraction. Once momentum is lost, it takes approximately 20 minutes to regain it. What is the solution? Turn off your email alerts and schedule times to monitor your email.

assisting others. Does it imply you cannot accomplish this? Of course not. It is a matter of doing so when the opportunity presents itself. In lieu of an open-door policy, for instance, "have specific communication periods—similar to "office hours"—when team members are permitted to ask questions and address issues."

Make it clear that your time is valuable.

John Hall, co-founder of Calendar, wrote on Success, "Because time is your most valuable asset, you cannot be willing to give it away without hesitation." John states, "It prevents you from putting your own goals and needs first." "It's as if you made deposits into everyone else's bank accounts but none into your own."

So, what signals are you sending that cause others to believe your time is not valuable? Here are four of the most common offenders:

Saying "yes" to every request. John writes, "If you accept every request that comes your way, you are putting the interests of others before your own." "Start saying 'no' more often," he instructs. It is the easiest way to begin achieving your objectives.

Easily becoming distracted. We had previously discussed email and office visits. However, social media, ambient commotion, and hunger are also potential distractions. Determine what causes you interruptions and when they occur so you can find ways to reduce them.

Being available 24/7. Smartphones contribute to this issue. However, the fact that we can always respond to a text or email does not imply that you should. Define when you are connected and when it is time to disconnect.

Disregarding schedule constraints. Did you schedule a 15-minute teleconference? Therefore, this is how long the call will last.

Permitting tardiness. Assume that a coworker or friend arrives 15 minutes late. Let them know that is unacceptable. "When someone disregards your time," John explains, "you lose time to concentrate on your goals."

What is the most important takeaway? Don't take leisure for granted. Enjoy it instead so that you can savor every minute of every day.

Similar to other nations, management in Russia reflects its history, culture, and social psychology. It is directly related to the country's socioeconomic structure.

Due to historical factors, our nation's economy is expanding at a rapid rate; all of our processes occur in shorter time intervals. During the Soviet era of Russian history, there was no private property, whereas the science of management experienced a worldwide expansion. Therefore, managers are now required to work more efficiently, and it is not surprising that the majority of them struggle with time management and scheduling. All Russian economists acknowledge that the efficient use of time is a necessary condition for any labor process, including managerial ones. Despite this, the problem of efficient time management has been either ignored or covered inadequately in the vast majority of management-related studies.

Currently, leaders can be divided into two groups: leaders of the old school, who operated in a planned economy and find it challenging to adapt to new circumstances. They prefer to continue working in the same manner as before.

The majority of new managers with training in foreign literature studied or trained abroad. They utilized the knowledge of Western managers and, as a result, differ little from their international peers. It is natural for them to prioritize the most effective use of their working time.

The economy of Russia is currently in transition. In a planned and market economy, the external environment is relatively stable, whereas businesses today operate in an environment that is continuously changing. This circumstance makes decision-making more difficult. Plans must be continuously revised. The manager's objectives are not always transparent and consistent. Multiple objectives, combined with the existence of diverse groups and interests, frequently result in conflicts. Inability to establish distinct and consistent objectives violates the very first stage of self-management. As a result, the planning and decision-making processes become more challenging (unexpected tasks arise, and it is impossible to explicitly prioritize).

As previously mentioned, the application of time management principles is associated with not only economic, but also social and psychological factors.

In our country, a significant portion of managers' time budgets are devoted to routine tasks. This suggests difficulties with the Russian delegation of managers. Many of them do not delegate routine tasks, either because their subordinates are already overburdened or because they believe they can perform the task more effectively themselves. As a result, the manager lacks sufficient time for truly vital and fruitful duties.

A further characteristic of the use of working time in Russian companies is the prevalence of cordial relationships between coworkers. Many people prefer to begin their workday with informal communication with coworkers rather than with the most important matters; a discussion of the provisions of the contract can easily transition into a friendly conversation.

In Russia, the image of a leader has developed as someone who is perpetually pressed for time, and the more time he lacks, the more important he appears. Some executives boast that they work 12 to 13 hour days as a sign of their commitment to their jobs. This objectively implies that a person cannot set priorities and organize his time effectively.

In essence, the effectiveness of a manager's time management depends on his personality, on whether he desires to streamline his activities by consistently applying the rules and principles of self-management to his work, as this does not require any supernatural efforts from a Russian manager or from a manager from any other country.

Chapter 5: How To Schedule A Perfect Week Ahead

What do I want to initiate that is not currently occurring?

What should I stop doing that is not beneficial?

What activities do I want to increase or decrease?

What activities align with my set of values? Who are those who do not?

Do I undertake too much? Not adequate?

As your action item, take stock of your current situation in any manner that is convenient for you. Determine how much time and effort each of your major life "buckets" requires. Then, simply enumerate three to five learnings from this activity.

Bonus: Redraw your inventory to reflect its appearance after one year.

DESIGNING YOUR PERFECT WEEK PLAN

Now that you have clarity about what you are doing now and what you want in the future, it is time to be creative.

Turn on your favorite music, recline on the couch, light a candle, and perhaps pour a glass of wine. Make the process of creating your ideal blueprint stimulating and enjoyable!

Choose Your Time Blocks First

Create a list of your various time blocks for different categories of activities, bearing in mind your inventory's values and priorities.

There may be duplication with your inventory. These should be a little more specific to the recurring tasks you perform throughout the week. You are free to use your imagination and select whatever makes sense to you.

Please note that you will only have your allotted time segments; this will not be graded.

As your action item, create a simple list of the essential time segments that you need now and want in the future.

Second, Select An Appropriate Calendar

The entire following week will be devoted to visualizing your plan on a calendar. Utilize the method that works best for you, whether it be on paper or on a computer.

I recommend maintaining your Ideal Week calendar separate from your regular calendar, regardless of the tool you use. You should occasionally refer to this calendar as a living, breathing document; you do not want it to yet become a part of your reality.

Your action item is to select a calendar utility or, if uncertain, to test out several.

Finally, map time blocks to your calendar.

Now is the moment to begin creating!

In lieu of a day-by-day calendar, I believe that a week's perspective should be presented at once. This will allow you to view your time within a broader context.

Begin by scheduling your weekly time blocks while contemplating the following questions:

How frequently must specific actions be performed?

What time do they take place?

How much time do we have?

These inquiries will provide clarity regarding the frequency, planning, and duration of your time blocks.

Keeping in mind that this is your ideal week and not an actual plan, you should be less concerned with specifics and more concerned with determining how much time and effort each activity will require. If your inner critic tells you that these things will never occur, pay heed and set it aside for now.

Chapter 6: Time Management Strategies For Achieving Your Objectives

Serious objective setting requires a laser-like focus on time management. Effective and efficient time management is one of the most valuable skills you can possess. You cannot accomplish your professional and personal objectives if you do not effectively manage your time. Yes, you may be able to make some progress, but the task will be challenging.

People who waste and neglect the limited time they have are painfully aware of how difficult it is to accomplish even moderately difficult objectives. Time is unquestionably the greatest leveler in existence. You have the same amount of time as everyone else, irrespective of age, income, gender, race, or religion. Your time is the same regardless of your financial status. All that matters is how well you manage your time.

Therefore, if you're serious about achieving your objectives, you'll need to be serious about averting distractions and becoming too engrossed in the bad habits you know you must break. Time-wasting activities must be eliminated, and their position must be filled by truly challenging tasks.

What is the key? Locate and implement an efficient time management system. There are numerous, and the choice is entirely yours. However, if you don't want to be one of the 92% of people who fail to achieve their long-term goals, you must be mindful of how you utilize the limited time you have on earth.

Ensure that you are setting objectives appropriately.

There is a right way to set objectives and a wrong way to do so. If you don't set your objectives properly, you won't have the appropriate targets, which will cause you to lose your way. However, when they are installed properly, the ceiling is the limit. Utilize the SMART goal-setting process to achieve your objectives. And when you do establish these objectives, ensure that you have strong, rooted motivations for achieving them.

Create an effective time management system.

Finding the right system to manage your time is one of the techniques for time management.

The quadrant system is probably the most successful time-management system. It organizes your tasks into four quadrants according to their importance and urgency. Things are either important or imperative, or they are neither. You should avoid neither (quadrant 4) of these duties; instead, you should focus on the not-so-urgent-but-important quadrant.

Monitor your schedule for seven days.

Spend the next seven days analyzing your time usage. What precisely are you doing? It is prudent to record it in a journal or on your phone. Divide the time into increments of 30 minutes or one hour. What have you achieved today? Was the time wasted? Is it a wise investment? Make a circle or a log in the quadrant where the action occurred if you're using the quadrant system. At the conclusion of seven days, total all the numbers. Where did you spend the most amount of time? Which quadrants do you prioritize? You could be astonished by the results.

Utilize MITS in the morning.

Perform your most essential responsibilities first thing in the morning. These are your most essential tasks (MITs) for the day. Getting these tasks accomplished will provide you with the most momentum for the remainder of the day.

Follow the 80-20 rule

The Pareto Principle, also known as the 80-20 Rule, is an additional effective time management technique. According to this formula, 20% of the results result from 80% of the effort. It also indicates that 20% of customers account for 80% of the sales. What is the key? Identify the 20% of efforts that yield 80% of the results, and then scale those efforts up.

Integrate pillar behaviors into your daily routine.

The keystone is the stone that holds the building's other stones in position. Similarly, keystone habits encourage the formation of new good habits and aid in the elimination of bad ones. Focusing on pillar habits will make habit formation much simpler, thereby improving your overall time management.

Schedule time for responding to correspondence.

During the day, disable email access. It is simple to become distracted when one's email inbox is cluttered. Make time to regularly peruse and respond to email. Someone will contact or text you if an emergency occurs. When you have your email open, however, these interruptions disrupt your mental rhythm and make it more challenging to refocus.

Eliminate objectionable conduct

The time we devote to our negative behaviors is one of the greatest dangers. It makes no difference if we watch a lot of Netflix, spend a lot of time on social media, play a lot of video games, or frequently go out drinking with friends. These toxic behaviors consume the limited time we have. Get rid of bad habits if you want to make the most of your time and accomplish significant life objectives.

Take frequent breaks while employed

52 minutes of labor should be followed by a 17-minute break. It is possible that you will not have the chance to do so. However, you should take frequent rests. This is particularly crucial if you are a self-employed entrepreneur. It is very easy to be operating on fumes without realizing it.

By taking frequent pauses, you can maintain optimal mental, emotional, and physical health.

daily, engage in meditation or exercise

You may not believe that daily meditation and exercise can improve your time management, but they will. You will notice a significant difference in your vitality, stamina, and mental clarity if you eliminate toxins from your life and take it seriously.

Evening to-do lists are created for the following day.

Make a list of tasks for the following day before heading to bed each night. You should evaluate your objectives and determine what you can do to achieve them. In this instance, it does not occur immediately. Time will be required. To-do lists are an excellent method for establishing daily objectives. Daily objectives are simpler to achieve, and they also help us achieve our long-term and larger objectives. Create an inventory of tasks.

When feeling down, seek out inspiration. When feeling down, consult YouTube, TED Talks, or any other source of inspiration you can discover. When one lacks motivation, it is difficult to maintain track of time. Find methods to reignite your passion by focusing on motivational content and seeking out individuals who have achieved great things.

Find a guide to assist you.

It is essential to locate a mentor. It is simple to become distracted and disheartened in the absence of guidance. When you can personally rely on someone who has been through the ringer and can assist you in achieving your objectives, it is easier to manage your time. Find a wise guide who can assist you on your voyage.

Disable social media app notifications

Constantly receiving notifications from social media applications is not an efficient use of your time. It is causing you considerable discomfort. Switch them off. You do not need to constantly receive notifications or know what your peers are doing. It is immaterial. The most essential thing is to relax and concentrate on your duties.

Organize and declutter

When there is a lot of debris around us, we lose concentration. We waste time when we are not attentive. To prevent this from occurring, you should tidy and organize. Don't attempt to do everything at once. Start with baby measures. Today, I only have one compartment.

Tomorrow, I will have a bookcase. The following day, a wardrobe. One per day only, sir. You gain self-assurance and become a warrior for order.

Chapter 7: Common Time Blocking Errors And Ways To Prevent Them

Although time blocking is intuitive in theory, it can be difficult to implement in practice. Here are a few tips to help you effectively implement the strategy (and avoid becoming a slave to your schedule):

Underestimating your time.
You'll get better at estimating how much time tasks require over time, but until you've honed your sensibilities, it's preferable to reserve a great deal of time for activities rather than almost none. Give yourself additional time to complete and transition between activities. You may create "contingent blocks" of time that you can use if you fall behind schedule.

Being unduly rigid.

Things will occur that will demolish your plans. However, keep in mind that your agreement is not an official contract; it is merely a guide to help you focus on what's important. Indeed, even productivity guru Cal Newport adjusts his schedule throughout the day by erasing unique time segments and replacing them with new plans as circumstances dictate.

Newport manages changes in his schedule by viewing it as a game: "This type of planning, as far as I'm concerned, resembles a chess game, with blocks of work being spread and arranged so that projects of all sizes all appear to click into completion with (barely sufficient time) to spare." Consider your time limits as a flexible method for testing yourself, rather than as rigid instruments for excusing yourself when you fall short.

3. overscheduling your time for relaxation.

Even though Elon Musk and Bill Gates are rumored to plan their days down to 5-minute increments, it is risky to overschedule your leisure time. Studies have demonstrated that planning recreation exercises has a "special housing impact" on the overall enjoyment of physical activity. Without a predetermined plan for how you'll employ that energy, you can deny yourself the opportunity to disengage and relax. It will give you the flexibility to decide more quickly what you need to do—call your companions to grab a drink? Consider this new Xbox game. Peruse? Whatever you decide to do, ensure that you reserve at least some of your spare energy.

Work in support of.

It may seem counterintuitive, but pauses are essential for improved time management. According to research, common pauses improve productivity, mental health, independent decision-making, and memory. In addition, skipping pauses can hasten fatigue and increase stress. Therefore, what does this have to do with time management? Higher levels of anxiety influence energy, exhaustion, insight, as well as work productivity and dedication. Thus, amusingly, working less (by taking more breaks) can help you accomplish more substantially more quickly.

Incorporate pauses into your schedule. Give yourself a chance to unwind after completing a responsibility. Enjoy smaller-than-usual respites to re-energize, such as a brief walk, a game of ping pong, some introspection, etc.

Determine how to say no.
You will never learn how to manage your time at work until you learn how to say no. You alone comprehend why you

have time, so if you wish to decline a request in order to concentrate on additional substantial activities, make it a point to do so. Moreover, if you undertake an endeavor that is manifestly doomed to fail, make it a point to abandon it.

Instead of completing a large number of activities that yield little to no value, focus on fewer endeavors that generate greater value. Remember the 80/20 rule, which states that 20% of your feedback accounts for 80% of your results. Center your endeavors as needs be. If you can't say no, delegate it. Although designating is a difficult skill to acquire, it can make all the difference in your time management. You've assembled a talented team, so determine which tasks you can delegate.

9. Obtain Coordination.
This tip must be included in your daily schedule if you wish to effectively manage your time. If your work area is littered with stacks of scattered

documents, locating the one you need will be akin to searching for a very elusive object. There are few things as perplexing as spending considerable time seeking for lost items. Also the means by which difficult muddle can reach the center.

The impact of seemingly inconsequential details is substantial. Create a framework for documenting reports. Remove messages you no longer require. Automate repetitive tasks or cycles whenever possible. Create frameworks for coordinating and completing tasks to increase your efficiency. Simply consider — you only need to do it once, but the benefits will last forever.

10. Wipe out interruptions.
Virtual entertainment, web browsing, coworkers, instant messages, and messaging are just a few of the many potential workplace interruptions. A crucial aspect of time management is being proactive about completing tasks. Close your entrance to reduce

disruptions. Close all tabs except the ones you are currently working on. Turn off alerting notifications and save your contacts for lunch.

Make infant progress. Identify your top two interruptions and concentrate on eliminating them for an extended period of time. In addition, remember that having enough sleep, drinking enough water, and eating well can all help you stay on track during a typical business day — especially during the midday slump.

Better time management requires skills, not tricks. No "favorable to tip" or scheduling device will magically solve your time management issues at the end of the day if you lack a solid foundation of time management skills.

The Harvard Business Survey identifies three essential abilities that distinguish successful time management from failure:

Realizing that your time is a limited resource and contemplating it accordingly.

Plan of action: arranging objectives, plans, schedules, and assignments for optimal time management.

Transformation: routinely evaluating how you spend your time while exercising, including adjusting to interruptions or changing requirements.

Utilize the aforementioned advice to assist you in developing these skills and establishing lasting, effective time management habits.

Chapter 8: Tips For Creating A Productive To-Do List

The accompanying list of ideas complements some effective methods for creating a workable daily schedule. If some of the ideas appear contradictory to others, this is because they are. It is anticipated that certain methods will resonate with particular readers. Accept those who labor for you.

Don't Put Too Much Weight on It

This is essential. If you pass this test, everything else will fall into order.

Be realistic in your assumptions and schedule estimates. Create a genuine schedule, not a fantasy schedule. Otherwise, you will spend the day behind schedule, acting erratically, and only frantically rushing to catch up. For will be able to observe how your proficiency declines as you become irritable and exhausted.

Consider what absolutely requires your attention, tasks that no one else can perform, and include them on your list. Since you've planned out your massive tasks, estimated how long they'll take, and determined when each step must be completed (haven't you?), write down the essential steps.

However, avoid using the regimen. You will find that there is no space on your to-do list for less important, optional, or even forgettable tasks if you include only the most crucial, must-do items. That is not an issue. Allow the list to aid you in getting organized, staying focused, and completing the essential tasks.

If, due to a supernatural occurrence, things take less time than anticipated, you should celebrate! You have provided yourself with an endowment of saved opportunity, which you are free to expend as you see fit.

To assist with observing rule number one, observe rule number two.

Exaggerate the travel duration. Consider the waiting time prior to the meeting, the time spent on hold, and the traffic reinforcement. Due to Murphy's Law, preparing for a potential traffic jam ensures that it will not occur, and you will arrive at your destination sooner than anticipated. Allowing yourself scarcely enough time for your outing guarantees a postponement. Currently, you are aware.

3. List Opportunities, Not Obligations

This pertains more to your mindset when creating the list than to the specific documentations on that list. You are posting assignments that you trust, require, and must complete during the day. You are not creating a blueprint for the rest of the universe, and your plans lack the force of natural law.

What happens if you do not accomplish everything on your list? What happens, for instance, if you wake up effectively too sick to even consider getting out of bed, much less face a jam-packed workday?

I'm not referring to a minor hoarse throat and headache that could keep you in bed on the weekend but not on a typical workday. In this manner, the not faking infection is simpler, as you don't need to choose whether or not to attempt to go to work, and you don't need to feel guilty about staying in bed while the rest of the world is conducting business. (Depending on your tolerance for pain and your level of responsibility, you may need to be near to insanity to attain this state.)

Let's say you're so exhausted that you can only lie flat on your back in bed for two days, and on the third you can barely walk around the house in your bathrobe and slippers. You miss a total of seven consecutive days of employment.

In the meantime, what happened to the items on your to-do list?

The events occurred without you. People determined they could survive another week without the quarterly report. You have 138 messages on voicemail (62 of which are from the same person), 178 messages (52 of which are duplicates of responses and responses to responses by various beneficiaries on a single inquiry), and a desk flooded with updates, faxes, and other unnatural disasters. You bring items home for a week in an endeavor to be captured.

That is terrible, but not so terrible. You didn't pass on. You did not lose a friend or relative. The development of the West did not halt. Government and business worked out how to proceed without you.

It's past due to respond to some of these urgent messages and emails, but it turns out they didn't require a response after all.

Try to remember this when you are generally healthy but falling behind on your day's duties.

Consider yourself to have had a dreadful day at work? Consider former Los Angeles Dodgers center fielder Willie Davis, who met his own misfortune during the 1965 World Series' second round against the Baltimore Orioles. Davis blew the game in the fifth inning, with the score tied 0-0 and the Dodgers' ace Sandy Koufax on the mound, by committing three errors in a single inning and recalling two for similar plays. The Dodgers never recovered, losing four consecutive games in the series.

After his outstanding performance, Davis was philosophical. "This is not my life," he told a massive radio and television audience. Additionally, it is not my significant other. Then why fret?"

Another baseball player and genius, Satchel Paige, said, "Don't look back. You may be acquiring something."

Planify Your Tasks

If you can set aside time in your schedule to complete a specific task, there is a much greater chance that you will actually complete it. You will be mentally prepared, intent on completing the task, and less prone to interruptions if it is planned with a beginning and conclusion. Particularly for challenging duties, scheduling a one-hour or even a half-hour time frame makes the task less intimidating.

5. Do not etch the list into stone

Your list must be adaptable if it is to be of genuine use to you. You must be able to change it, deviate from it, turn it on its head, add to it, crumple it up, and toss it in the recycling bin if it's truly going to help.

Find a flexible organization that suits your needs. Choose the lattice if you prefer a multifaceted matrix framework with squares that rotate like clockwork throughout the day. Assuming you maintain your list on a PDA, replete with contractions that indicate priority, that is acceptable. Start scrawling if colored pencil on butcher paper is more your style.

Do not endeavor to fit an arrangement; none of them are excellent. Try some or all of them until you discover or create a solution that works for you.

6. Arrange Artfully

Ensure that the primary tasks are completed before you drown in a sea of relative random data. Respond to the email first assuming that it is the most important item on your agenda. If it isn't, plan it for later in the day, or if at all possible, set aside a couple of periods consistently to deal with email. Try not to do it first simply on the grounds that it's there, requesting your consideration, or on the grounds that it's relatively simple, or on the grounds that you've gotten into the propensity of doing it first. It is too simple to believe that you can keep up with an extensive email discussion on a small project, only to discover that your morning has been wasted.

Try to vary your pace by alternating difficult and simple, lengthy and brief, positions requiring creative thought with repetition capacities. Alternate exercises so frequently that they remain novel. Assume a mentally taxing position when you are generally prepared and alert. The large majority of us understand this to mean first thing. If you save them for a later date, you are conceding that you will not deal with them.

Turn Large Jobs into Small Jobs.

When large projects are involved, it is essential to identify and limit (separate and conquer) the task's components. Indeed, it is essential to break down a large project into smaller tasks in order to understand the steps involved and what lies ahead in order to achieve the larger objective.

If one of your tasks is writing a product development plan, for example, and you know how much time and effort it will require, defining the components of the plan will make it significantly more manageable. You might avoid the task if it required you to "write a product development plan," but "gather serious information" is considerably more amenable. By devoting only thirty minutes to this step, you are guaranteed to complete it and obtain a sense of accomplishment toward the overall objective.

8. Include Scheduled Breaks, Time-Outs, and Small Rewards

The majority of us reserve "rest" for last, if we plan it at all. When we reach that stage, assuming we reach it, it will no longer be possible to help us.

If you do not include lie on the rundown, it will not occur. For, include a commencing and ending point on the rundown. Additionally, do not save it for last. Before you become excessively agitated or depleted, schedule your rest so that it will benefit you the most. Brief breaks at opportune moments will assist you in maintaining a consistent, proficient work tempo.

 Instead of waiting until the end of the day for 15 minutes of pleasure reading, schedule three five-minute reading intervals throughout the day. You may need to schedule a game of catch with your child or a meander through the neighborhood with your partner. You could use software that reminds you of your scheduled pauses so that you do not need to remember them.

Glasser's Corollary of Murphy's Law best describes this expression of semi-genuine alertness: If, of the seven hours you spend at work, six hours and 55 minutes are spent working at your work area, and the remaining time is spent tossing the bull with a coworker, the time at which your manager will walk in and ask what you're doing is not fixed to within five minutes.

9. Schedule Long-Term Personal Objectives

You are aware that you need to do some serious financial planning. You are aware that you should have a valid will. For the foreseeable future, you should establish a system for property maintenance and repair.

If you know all of this but never seem to get to it, put it on your schedule. Moreover, if you plan these objectives in a reasonable amount of advance, you will be much more likely to achieve them.

Be Willing to Abandon the List

The essayist and instructor Ellen Hunnicutt tells her students, "If you only write the planned story, you miss the story that is revealed."

The same holds true for the story of your existence. The most important thing you do all day, all year, or even your entire existence may never appear on any daily agenda or day organizer. Never become so productive that you lose sight of life's opportunities - the chance encounter, the sudden inspiration.

Not all surprises are terrible disasters. It simply appears that way on occasion.

Read "A List," one of Arthur Loebel's fantastic Frog and Toad stories, for a fantastic depiction of the dangers of developing a list compulsion (which, at this point, undoubtedly requires its own twelve-venture projects and support groups).

One morning, Toad admits, "I have completed the necessary tasks." "I will jot them all down on a list so I can recall them"

He records "awaken" and, realizing that he has completed it, crosses it off - a tremendous energy booster.

Other activities include "getting dressed," "eating breakfast," and "taking Frog for a walk."

A disaster occurs when a cyclone snatches the script from Toad's hands, leaving him unprepared for acting without the script to guide him.

The tale of Toad has an upbeat conclusion. You will merely need to make time to read it for yourself.

You Do Not Need to Make a List

The daily schedule is a tool. Procedures for creating an effective summary are concepts, not mandates. If they are helpful, adhere to them, adapting and modifying them to your own circumstances and tendencies. create your own type of list, or don't create a list at all, if they do not help. If you find yourself spending an inordinate amount of time creating and revising the list, or if you never refer to the list once it's complete, the daily schedule may not be for you. You won't have "bombed using time effectively." You will have examined a cycle that benefits some individuals but not others, and determined that you fall into the "not others" category.

Chapter 9: Some Suggestions To Reduce Distractions And Improve Concentration

Increasing your focus and completing your most important duties may be facilitated by the following suggestions.

Prepare your plan the evening before: To ensure a productive day, you may wish to jot down the two most essential tasks that must be completed. The presence of two tasks may be due to the fact that the first task takes less time than anticipated or requires the completion of another task before it can be initiated.

The second responsibility exists in case the first fails. Start with these responsibilities.Before opening your email, responding to your phone calls, or reading your social media feeds, any of these tasks can rapidly consume your morning.

Please terminate the Distractions:
When you search for information beforehand, you reduce the likelihood that it will interfere with your ability to concentrate on your task. It is advised that you disable all notifications from the applications operating on your smartphone and desktop computer. Consider only monitoring your email four times per day and responding to each inquiry once. You can reduce the number of things that distract you and improve your concentration by taking control of your electronic devices, as opposed to letting technology control you.

This information will have a unique significance for each and every small business owner. The attire, the chair, the music, the temperature of the room, and the location of the job may all affect a person's comfort level. If you are familiar with the types of environments that enable you to feel comfortable while also allowing you to concentrate, it may be easier for you to maintain your focus throughout the workday.

Regular meditation may make it simpler for your mind to let go of distracting thoughts and focus on a single subject. Give yourself three to five minutes per day to sit still and be silent to get started. Cover your eyes with your hands and count to thirty-four.

This may initially appear difficult because the mind tends to wander to other ideas, particularly those that may prevent one from reaching the objective of 34. You may be able to get back on track by abandoning this notion without judging yourself and beginning to count from the beginning. Notate any feelings or sensations that arise while performing this exercise. This is a procedure that is more difficult than it may initially appear.

Set Objectives That Are More Attainable: Ambitious goals are great material for motivational speeches, but they do little to help people zero in on and complete the tasks that matter. Consider dividing your goals into smaller, more manageable chunks so that you can attain them more quickly. As a result, it may be necessary to concentrate for a brief period of time, which may indicate that the likelihood of completing the task is increased.

Seven to nine hours of sleep per night is recommended for healthy individuals. In an effort to complete more tasks, many small business owners forgo sleep in order to continue working extended hours. Even more worrisome is the fact that this "sleep debt" may accrue over an extended period of time. A lack of sleep may impair a person's ability to sustain focus and perform tasks with the highest degree of proficiency possible. A sufficient amount of sleep will likely improve both your concentration and your general health.

Use Visual Reminders: The phrase "Focus, Focus, Focus" appears in three distinct locations on the top of the computer display at my place of employment. When I am having difficulty adhering to a task or want to avoid it to check my email or social media, I glance at this reminder and repeat the three phrases aloud. This indicator is extremely beneficial to me!

Giving Yourself a Reward: Delaying gratification is a technique that can help individuals maintain their focus on completing a task. Select the activity and the individualized reward (getting food, checking social media, calling a friend, etc.) that will serve as a direct motivator before commencing. This will permit you to test it out.

You may discover that you are able to concentrate better after getting up and moving around, or even better, after exiting the office. Even a brief break from one's work, in the form of a stroll outside, can be beneficial for the body and psyche. Taking a brief pause and then returning to work refreshed could help you complete the next task more efficiently.

Turn It On and Have Fun: Activities that do not require mental effort, such as screen time, can help free up mental capacity so that you can focus on a new activity later. Consider spending at least 30 minutes per day engaging in some form of physical activity, such as going to the gym, going for a run or a bike ride, playing sports, doing puzzles, or playing chess. Always remember that a healthy body is necessary for a healthy mind. When a person's body is ill or their mind is miserable, concentration may be difficult.

Chapter 10: Proceed Wherever Your Energy Leads You.

Spending time with family and friends or taking a meander through the local park are all viable options for filling one's day. You may even read several chapters from your book. Initially, it does not appear to be a productive method of conducting business. In contrast, despite how indirect it may appear, it is actually quite productive. Instead of drawing out your days due to lack of motivation, you are more likely to accomplish more with better results if you follow your energy.

When you take a break from the hustle and commotion of your home-based business, your zeal is rekindled and you're eager to get back to work. You might even take advantage of this opportunity to obtain a degree that will eventually make you more valuable to your employer. When you have an urgent need to think, develop, design, promote, network, strategize, or publish, you can accomplish a great deal in a brief amount of time.

Today's business environment is becoming increasingly demanding. The proprietors of home-based businesses are attempting to comply by spending more time in the "office," but this practice frequently backfires.

Both business proprietors and their employees are becoming exhausted, estranged, and ill. They are leaving the group in search of employment in environments with improved working conditions.

Working lengthy, arduous hours at a desk is inefficient due to the fact that time is a limited resource. Personal energy, however, can be replenished indefinitely. You can effectively develop physical, mental, and emotional resilience by regularly engaging in a variety of modest energy-recharging rituals. Simple rituals may include pausing at regular intervals to express gratitude, setting a time limit on distractions, or simply devoting more time to the tasks you find most pleasurable and productive. Your bottom line will unquestionably benefit from your consistent efforts to replenish your vitality.

MATTER OF ENERGY

Every day has a unique amount of vitality. On occasion, you cannot wait to begin the day. On such days, you can rise with a positive disposition, grab your briefcase, and proceed to work.

There has been a great deal of research conducted on the topic of physical energy. According to studies, regular exercise and proper nutrition are essential for maintaining physical vitality. Additionally, it is crucial to get sufficient slumber. You must allow your body to regenerate the energy expended during exercise and daily activities. This is the only method to develop and maintain energy, strength, and vitality effectively.

When your energy levels are low, you feel less confident, less enthusiastic, and rapidly develop a low sense of self-worth. Low levels of physical vitality will negatively impact your performance on work-related tasks.

Your mind and body are in dire need of periods of relaxation and rest in order for you to regain your customary business-mindedness. Here are a few measures you can take to develop and maintain adequate physical energy, allowing you to perform better and accomplish more in your home-based business:

Take the time to consume a modest snack or meal approximately every three hours.

Each night, go to bed earlier to ensure you are receiving enough sleep.

Reduce the quantity of alcohol you consume on a daily basis. In general, no more than three beverages per day is advised.

Exercise is essential. At least three times per week, you should engage in some form of cardiovascular activity, such as running. You should also integrate strength training into your routine at least once per week. Learn to recognize the indicators of low energy, such as excessive yawning, slight hunger, restlessness, and difficulty concentrating.

Every hour and a half to two hours, get up and move around your workspace. Give your body and mind time to recuperate by taking a vacation.

To be successful in the business world, you must concentrate on being your best self and doing whatever it takes to attain your objectives. The best method to accomplish this is to relax and rejuvenate your mind and body.

CONSCIOUS ENERGY

It is essential to recognize that while you may be feeling physically exhausted, your spirit may also be exhausted. Taking care of your mental health is just as important for your physical vitality as exercising and consuming a balanced diet. A lifestyle that inspires you and provides you a sense of inner purpose is essential.

an enhanced perspective and sense of self. When your emotional energy is intact, you will be better equipped to perform at the profession you enjoy because you will be more in touch with your business.

Neglecting to nourish your emotional energy may result in a lack of motivation, which could be detrimental to the success of your home-based business. The following recommendations will help you maintain a healthy level of emotional energy:

Put your own requirements first and live for yourself. For instance, if you want to invest in a business strategy that seasoned veterans are afraid to attempt, you should do so if you have the means and motivation to do so. When you spend your emotional energy attempting to make everyone else content, you will effectively deplete the emotional energy you need to run a successful business.

Surround yourself with supportive, business-focused individuals who share your vision. Avoid miserable individuals who spend their days nagging, complaining, and harping on their issues. These individuals will drain the vitality from your company. Work with individuals who inspire and motivate you to perform at your best, and who are themselves motivated to perform well.

Ensure that your agenda always includes innovative and profound ideas. Make elaborate plans for your next vacation or something else that can serve as an objective. Having an objective or reward to anticipate will motivate and inspire you to perform at the highest level. Your objectives should motivate you to get up and go to work every day. Hope converts directly to emotional energy; working toward a goal will not only increase your level of happiness, but it will also motivate you to continue your good deeds so that you continue to reap the benefits.

Exist in the present moment. Forget about failed commercial ventures from the past. Focus on what you intend to do next and in the future with your home-based business. It is impossible to plan for everything; therefore, you must ensure that your plan is sufficiently adaptable to allow you to achieve your objectives.

When you are feeling anxious, irritable, apprehensive, or impatient, abdominal breathing can help to calm these negative emotions.

Pay it forward by expressing your gratitude to your coworkers and business partners through specific emails, notes, or phone calls.

Approach challenging situations with a fresh viewpoint, learn from your mistakes, and develop as a result of your experience.

Remember that you control your own fate, which will be much simpler for you to do now that you've learned to increase and maintain your emotional energy.

MIND ENERGY

Mental stress is the nagging voice in your head that reminds you to meet deadlines and prepare for meetings; however, if stress is not managed, the negative impact on your mental energy could substantially impair your ability to perform well at work. Effective tension management is the key to success.

Here are some tips to help you manage your stress and re-energize your mind so you can complete more duties for your home business:

You are not required to be productive every day. Delegate your responsibilities to simplify the situation.

Set limits for yourself and do not be afraid to say "no" Helping to organize a work-from-home conference at the town hall is one thing; if you need time to work on your own business, do not agree to plan the entire event.

Document everything. It has been demonstrated that keeping a journal can significantly improve one's daily existence. By writing down your stressful emotions, you free up significant portions of your brain to concentrate on more essential matters.

Develop a positive outlook by incorporating humor into your daily routine. Subscribing to "joke of the day" emails or displaying a humorous image on the office wall are two ways to inject humor into the workplace. When the going gets rough, the straightforward things that make you laugh in life will keep you motivated.

Connect with others and do not be afraid to seek assistance when necessary. Do not waste time attempting to figure out the newly installed software when someone more qualified can complete the task more quickly. There is no disgrace in requesting assistance or advice.

Take regular rests. Allow your mind and body time to refresh, particularly when working on difficult or time-consuming duties.

When working on duties that require a great deal of concentration, you can reduce the likelihood of interruption by avoiding email and phone calls. Set aside periods throughout the day to respond to email and voicemail.

Determine each evening, before leaving work, what the most difficult task for the following day will be, and make it your top priority when you return to work the following day.

Chapter 11: Declutter Your Days

These activities have the extraordinary capability to waste countless hours of your time. Numerous experts recommend keeping note of how much time you spend on such activities each week to determine where your time has gone. Because these pastimes can be time-consuming and addictive, you should monitor how much time you devote to them if you want to improve your time management skills. Then, devise a plan to reduce or restrict your usage, including turning off your devices at specific times to maximize the effectiveness of your full attention.

It's not that these pastimes or technologies are bad or incorrect; many have practical applications or are enjoyable ways to decompress. You also require leisure time, but you must determine how much more time you wish to devote to these pursuits. This is effective time management. If you are active and want to accomplish your objective, you will have to reduce or abandon these activities. Consider how much time you expend on such activities and how it affects your ability to pursue your life goals.

We struggle with this because we want to assist our colleagues and friends with their requests. There are demands from all parties, and we wish to be of assistance. It is challenging to say no. However, there are only 24 hours in a day, and no matter how hard we try, we will not be able to complete our to-do lists before going to bed.

God grants us a limited amount of time each day, and regardless of how much you want to do or how much you want to serve others, you can only accomplish so much. Avoid overcommitting and overextending yourself. This adds a great deal of tension, prevents you from producing, and causes you to feel overwhelmed. Studies indicate that individuals who are truthful about the difficulty, complexity, and duration of a task are more likely to complete it.

Make a concerted effort to be truthful regarding the amount of time necessary to complete a project, whether you would accept another assignment, and whether you would meet the deadline. Utilize a well-maintained to-do list to keep track of what you already have on your schedule. Lastly, you must be willing to acknowledge "No" when necessary. Saying no to tasks that could overwhelm you will preserve your ability to complete essential, high-quality work, maintain focus, and be sufficiently refreshed to partake in conversations, creative problem-solving, etc. in the long run.

Regardless of how adept you believe you are at managing your time, you can undoubtedly improve. After six hours of nonstop labor, some of us are contented. This does not, however, imply that we were truly productive. It is not effective time management to study for hours on end or to multitask; it is about making the most of your time. You can accomplish significantly more by working intelligently (not harder) and complementing your natural focus, thereby completing tasks to a higher standard and gaining more time.

3.2 Setting Your Work Priorities

Once you have a substantial amount of daily task, you will need a system to keep track of everything. Prioritizing is the process of determining what you have been doing first and in what order of importance. Knowing how to effectively prioritize your responsibilities will save you time at work.

Prioritizing involves determining the order in which duties must be completed based on their relative importance. This method may help you organize your time more effectively. This teaches you to prioritize important tasks, meet deadlines, and have significantly more opportunities to complete larger projects. Prioritization abilities may enable you to complete more work in less time.

Even during the workday, tasks are frequently prioritized (or not) based on the needs of others rather than the immediacy of deadlines. This can also occur in our personal lives, where less time is spent on truly essential tasks and more time is spent being "busy." This can be changed by successfully prioritizing jobs with purpose according to future goals, ensuring that each work you do adds value, and preventing unimportant tasks from cluttering your schedule. Utilizing prioritization strategies enables you to make the most of your time at work and at home, thereby profoundly altering the course of your day.

Identify the Most Critical Tasks
Prioritize the items on your to-do list based on their importance. This may

depend on your weekly objectives, consumer needs, or coworker demands. Before moving on to other responsibilities, you can focus on a due-today research report.

Create a chart of your duties.
Once you've determined which tasks are the most essential, incorporate them into your schedule. Examining your daily to-do list can make it easier to prioritize your time. You may find that having a reminder of each task you must complete helps you to focus solely on them. Completing them may also provide a sense of accomplishment.

Establish Limits
After you have completed your day's responsibilities, you can further prioritize by selecting specific times to focus on your task. There may be coworkers who routinely call, email, or visit your office to discuss non-urgent matters. It is acceptable to let them know that you are occupied with assignments and will contact them later.

You may advise them not to disturb you in the mornings, but that you would be happy to communicate with them later.

Updating your email replying schedule so that others are aware of the times of day when you respond to emails is another way to prioritize your time. Setting aside specific periods of uninterrupted work time may help you concentrate more effectively and complete more duties.

Allow for Possible Distractions.
It is normal to become diverted throughout the day, whether you have shifted your focus to another task or are responding to a colleague. Throughout the day, you may also require rest and refocus intervals. It may be easier to incorporate interruptions into your schedule if you accept that they will occur. You can even schedule your intervals, such as a ten-minute refreshment break midday and a fifteen-minute workout in the evening.

Utilize technology to your benefit.
Several productivity tools are now available to help you maintain focus and keep up with technological advancements. Installing an application that keeps track of your time spent on a specific task enables you to monitor your productivity. A timer can also help you concentrate on your work and plan pauses. For instance, you can set your clock for an hour of labor followed by a five-minute break.

One task at a time should be given priority.
It is tempting to multitask in order to accomplish more, but it is best to focus on one task at a time. This technique will ensure that you maintain complete concentration on the task at hand, allowing you to complete it swiftly before moving on to the next item on your to-do list. Because you are not distracted by other responsibilities, you have a higher chance of producing high-quality work.

Utilize a scheduling application.
Create an inventory of everything that is due in the following month to help you prioritize your obligations. Determine daily responsibilities by completing each week and the end of the following month. This can be recorded on a spreadsheet, and the activities can then be scheduled in a calendar. Setting deadlines for your assignments may aid in concentration and productivity.

Delegate Responsibilities
If you can delegate tasks or divide responsibilities with coworkers, you can create a weekly to-do list and delegate specific tasks to others. Determine which tasks others could perform without your supervision and delegate them to coworkers so that you can focus on pressing matters. This enables you to prioritize tasks that require immediate attention.

How do you spend your spare time? At times, you may feel like all you do is labor. It was not exaggerated. On average, adults devote one-third or more of their lives to their careers. You spend your time away from work traveling, doing housework, caring for your children, or conducting other routine maintenance.

Time constraints are a significant source of stress for many individuals. You experience anxiety and irritability when you are overwhelmed with tasks and unsure of where to start. These emotions impede your ability to reason and make decisions, preventing you from acting effectively. As a result, you will lose precious time.

Wouldn't it be great if you could organize your time effectively? However, upon reflection, no one could do it. No one has the ability to alter fate or travel back in time. "Time management" is a science fantasy concept. People can concentrate their efforts on what genuinely matters. This will increase your confidence and enable you to manage your anxiety levels.

Setting a goal allows for improvement over time.
Most authors on personal growth and self-development focus on continuous improvement. And for those unfamiliar with the concept, continuous improvement is making minimal efforts toward development as frequently as possible in order to become the person you want to be.
The goals you set for yourself will eventually shape you into the kind of man you want to be. They will change your character. As you establish a target for such a level of development, your objectives can help you monitor your progress. Self-motivation enables you to determine where you started, where you've been, and how far you still need to go. The primary objective can then serve as benchmarks and checkpoints to determine your progress toward your most important goals!

Goals Increase Happiness.

Believe us when we say that the feeling of accomplishment you receive from achieving goals can be both motivating and addictive (in a good way)! The serotonin released upon achieving a goal functions as a special reward for the brain, motivating us to continue striving. Having clearly defined goals will help reduce anxiety in your daily life, particularly if you adhere to them, work proactively towards achieving them, and surpass your initial estimates.

Moreover, our goals provide us with a target to strive for the things we desire most. Instead of advancement for progression, you can see where you're going! This is immensely more satisfying. Consider an extended car trip you took as a child. Every twenty minutes, you inquired, "Are we still there?" The journey appeared to last forever.

You risk undertaking the journey if you do not even know your destination. Mindless wandering is not particularly enjoyable. Goals make us feel good about the path we're following.

Goals Provide Guidance.

Goals provide direction, which is one reason they are so important. When you have clearly defined objectives, making crucial decisions becomes much simpler. You should not expend mental energy contemplating certain options that do not align with your objectives.

If your monthly goal is to lose 2 pounds and you are out for a nice meal, the choice between a fatty hamburger and a chicken salad is evident. In a formal setting, it is simple to choose between assisting your supervisor in creating a presentation for a meeting and having coffee with a friend if your goal is to advance your career.

Setting goals in this manner allows you to put your judgment on autopilot, which has the wonderful dual effect of making you more likely to achieve your goals and giving you more time and energy to concentrate on the more proactive actions required to achieve them.

4.2 Setting SMART Objectives

Do you often feel as though you are exerting great effort but making little progress? If you examine your abilities and accomplishments over the past five or ten years, you may not observe any growth. Perhaps you have difficulty imagining what you will accomplish in the future years.

Many individuals spend their lives moving from job to job or rushing around in an effort to accomplish more while achieving little. Developing SMART objectives helps to concentrate your efforts, maximize the use of your time and abilities, and increase your chances of achieving your life goals.

Goals are essential to all aspects of business life because they provide direction, motivation, clarity, and significance. A unique objective is utilized to assist in goal planning. SMART is an acronym for:
- Specialized
- Measurable
- Attainable
- Reasonable

- Timely

Consequently, a SMART goal incorporates all of these elements to help you achieve your objectives and increase your likelihood of success.

Setting objectives can help you achieve the career you desire. You can choose how to use your resources and time to achieve maximum success by establishing goals and a strategy for reaching them. If you do not have any objectives, it can be difficult to determine how to pursue a specific job, pay increase, or other milestone.

When you set an objective for yourself, you should include all the necessary steps for attainment.

Specific

Be as specific as possible regarding your objectives. The more specific your objective, the greater your understanding of the necessary steps to achieve it. Unless your goal is distinct and direct, you won't be able to focus or feel sufficiently motivated to achieve it.

If you wish to change your major, your objective statement should never contain deceptive language. Be explicit in your language, stating precisely what you intend to achieve and the actions you intend to take to achieve it. In other words, have a defined objective in view. For example, if you wish to become a physician, you will need to modify your subject areas. Determine which classes you should drop and which you should continue, and then contact the relevant officials for assistance.

Measurable

If your goal is to lead a design team for a new software company, you could measure your progress by the number of management positions you've applied for or the number of conversations you've had. Setting up checkpoints along the voyage will allow you to evaluate and modify your route as needed. Continue to reward yourself in small but significant ways whenever you achieve your objectives.

Your objective must be quantifiable. Something that can be measured and whose growth can be monitored. Have you been able to alter any of your courses to move closer to your aim of becoming a physician? Have you acquired the prerequisites for the course? Define your goals to track your progress

Achievable

Have you settled on a realistic and attainable objective for yourself? Setting goals that can be accomplished within a reasonable period of time will improve mood and concentration. Using the example of leading an engineering team, you must be aware of the necessary qualifications, knowledge, and skills. Before you begin working towards an objective, you should consider whether you can achieve it immediately or if you need to take additional preparatory steps.

Relevant

Evaluate the significance of your objectives before setting them. Each of your objectives must be consistent with your values and long-term goals. Reconsider an objective if it does not contribute to your ultimate objectives. Consider why the objective is important to you, how achieving it will benefit you, and how it can help you achieve your long-term goals.

Assume you realized in the middle of the semester that your chosen major did not correlate with your goal of becoming a doctor. You want the relevance of your classes to be at the forefront of your course selections now that you are prepared to establish meaningful goals. Maintain your focus on the ultimate objective.

Time-based

What is your intended due date? A deadline may improve your disposition and help you prioritize your duties. For example, if you wish to advance to a more senior position, you can establish a six-month deadline. Consider the fact that you have not achieved your objective. Your schedule may have been arbitrary, you may have encountered unanticipated obstacles, or your goal may be unattainable.

4.3 Three Principles

There are only 24 hours in a day, and no matter who you are or how hard you work, you will never be able to gain additional time because you have a fixed time limit that is the same for everyone. Despite this, some individuals accomplish far more in the same amount of time than others. How do you believe it's feasible? Have you previously heard of the three Ps of time management?

Consider a number of factors if you want to improve your organizational skills. Understanding how you spend all of your time is a useful starting point. Then you will be able to identify undesirable behaviors and learn how to eliminate them. Here are some strategies and techniques for using three-P management to accomplish more and be more productive: planning, prioritization, and execution.

Planning

We must pay close attention to a strategic plan because it enables us to manage everything with greater efficiency. "If you do not even make a plan, you will fail," the saying goes. If you don't plan, you won't know everything you need to know about your employment. You could be surprised, face unanticipated obstacles, neglect deadlines, and jeopardize your reputation if you are unprepared. This can be annoying, confusing, and intimidating. You must comprehend the significance of the plan. You may not see immediate benefits from preparation, but consider the cost of not doing so. Spend nearly 15 minutes per day preparing for the following day.

Thus, you will know precisely what you have been doing while conscious, and you will feel as though you have accomplished everything by the end of the day. The first stage is to write things down instead of keeping them in mind. Everything should be recorded on paper or in an Excel spreadsheet. Incorporate your daily responsibilities into your daily plan.

Set aside a certain amount of time for each task and estimate how much time it will take, but be reasonable. Additionally, limit your activities to a single activity per action. Will you instead concentrate on the newsletter's design, formatting, or text? Not the outcome, but each activity must be recorded. So, you have documented your obligations and scheduled time to complete them. What is subsequent? Which assignment should we complete first? There is only so much time in a day, so to be more efficient, we must prioritize the tasks that will yield the greatest benefit. This implies that you must prioritize and understand which tasks must be completed and ranked appropriately.

Prioritization

Try contemplating it. Which of your daily responsibilities would you rank as the most productive? Alternatively, which occupation is the most productive in terms of time? After identifying the most important tasks, consider the time allotted for each activity, and then seek for the second most important task, the third most important task, and so on. The work can be subdivided into multiple categories. These duties are essential and must be completed, but if you are constantly putting out fires, don't forget about other important but non-urgent responsibilities.

Examine the following list of activities to ensure that your priorities are always in order.

- Important but not Essential

These require action, which, while not required to be taken promptly, must be taken at some point. This will consume the majority of your vitality. These tasks are essential but unimportant and require immediate attention. This occurs when you agree to an excessive number of activities for others or when you are continuously distracted. Delete your emails, dust your workstation, and other diversions are frequent examples of busywork, but they are unquestionably worthwhile at times.

- Immediate

Phone calls, presentations, conferences, and other interruptions are examples of things that are not especially significant but are treated as such. But sometimes you just want to do the things you want to do rather than concentrating on other things. You will perform well with others if you can identify and reduce or eliminate such problems.

- Significant

After that, you have a variety of essential tasks, including networking, relationship building, posting on social networking sites, and blogging. While both are essential to the operation of your company, neither is indispensable.

- Time Wasters

Chitchat, Twitter, the Internet, political debate, and local gossip are examples of activities that dissipate time. These tasks are neither essential nor imperative and should be deferred until off-peak hours.

- Performance

You must execute the planned and prioritized tasks. You must devote one hundred percent of your focus to the task at hand. It must be accomplished devoid of interruptions or diversions. Close your inbox and power down your mobile device. Remove any disturbances that have come to your attention. This increases productivity while also enhancing the quantity and quality of work. You may be astonished at how much you can accomplish if you focus on one task at a time. Also, remember to pay attention to your vitality (how you think) and complete essential tasks because you are more vigilant and energized. Remember that planning, priority, and performance are the most important factors.

Chapter 12: Effective Time Routines

You're known as the punctual one at work and among your peers due to your consistent adherence to time. The time practices you adopt today and in the days, months, and years to come are intended to work in your favor so that you can experience significant life changes as you travel.

You are not intended to feel at any point on this journey that this is a form of punishment that you cannot enjoy. In fact, as you develop these routines, they should help you maximize your use of time, allowing you to reap the benefits of your efforts since you will now have time for all the things you value in life.

Understanding the Power of Time Your conscious and subconscious mind will play a crucial role in making this second nature to you over the course of the next few weeks as you work to change your time habits and rest habits. By developing a set of good practices, you will be able to avoid wasting time and instead use it to your advantage. Thus, you are able to accommodate everything you deem essential in your existence. Remember that the purpose of this article is not to make you work less in areas of your life in which you have already invested time, money, and effort. Instead, the objective is to have you divide your time equally and then maximize each division, so that if you feel that certain aspects of your life require more attention, you can find opportunities and methods to improve them without having to work harder.

Prioritize the most essential task at hand when establishing and practicing time management habits, as this will require the most of your attention and focus. Everyone's attention span is unique and varies throughout the day. But it is your responsibility to use the time of day when you can concentrate and focus the most to complete the tasks that matter most and have the greatest potential to improve your circumstances.

Consider that you are working to increase your business's assets or revenues through increased marketing. This is something you would do during your most productive hours of the day, as it will aid you in achieving greater success. My focus and concentration are at their peak when I first wake up in the morning, so I prioritize working on my business during this time of day over all other activities. I am aware that this is the factor that will have the greatest impact on my life, so I devote my mornings to focusing on it. In essence, you should examine your individual schedule to determine the most productive times of the day.

It is impractical to strive to be productive throughout the entire day. When you feel the least able to concentrate throughout the day, give yourself time to recover by taking breaks. If you develop the unhealthy habit of constantly pushing yourself to the limit, even when your body warns you to halt, you may end up exhausting yourself to death. Despite the fact that this may not alarm you at the moment, you must realize that when you are not at your best, everything you do thereafter will be of the lowest quality. This will no longer be effective or efficient, leaving you unproductive, fatigued, and burned out.

What Should Breaks Look Like?

Consider pauses necessary for rest and recuperation. Ensure that you are doing this correctly by allowing yourself time to unwind and realign your mind, body, and spirit. Here are some constructive break options you can consider for this purpose:

• Reading a lot so you can learn new things often • Meditating regularly • Practicing yoga • Avoiding the habit of remaining seated for long periods of time • Giving yourself a minimum of 15 minutes of moderate to fast-paced exercise daily • Spending time outdoors • Adding plant-based foods to your food diet • Getting yourself involved in voluntary work for organizations or activist groups • Fueling your passions and pursuing career paths that will be meaningful to you • Listening to music as often as you can • Exercising gratitude and appreciation for all that you have • Being kind to yourself and others • Getting enough sleep every night • Developing a beauty routine to detoxify your body • Learning to let go of little things • Learning to slow down when your body tells you to • Getting rid of sources that cause you to stress • Avoiding gossip and unnecessary drama • Laughing as often as you can • Traveling a lot so you can learn and explore new cultures • Forgiving yourself of past mistakes • Opting for natural ways to treat yourself

Time spent on a productive break will maximize the use of the allocated time for this break. Even during vacations, time should be used productively. This is how you maximize your performance and output at various periods of the day.

Your Takeaway

The tasks with the greatest potential to help you achieve your objective must receive the most time and attention. You have a limited amount of time, so prioritize this by performing the actions with the highest potential for profit. Determine what you are generally interested in doing with your time and ensure that it relates to your personal success and satisfaction. Negative events, individuals, and/or experiences are a waste of time and will make you miserable. Use your time only for the good. Consequently, you will feel improved.

Chapter 13: Consider Your Time And Energy Resources

The initial portion of the thread states that you should not dwell on the past or future. The past is deceased and buried; all that is left are fragments of memory that you cling to. Additionally, you may stop the recycling procedure at any time. Because regardless of how hard you try to relive a past experience, it is no longer accurate. Furthermore, the future is nonexistent and uncertain.

When you allow your mind and attention to be focused on the present moment, you attain the realm of timelessness, which Eckhart Tolle calls the eternal Now.

In contrast, time is the most valuable resource in existence. It cannot be transferred or refunded. Time that has already been spent cannot be recycled, and time that has already been squandered cannot be recovered. Therefore, no one, including yourself, should be permitted to unduly utilize your time. People often state that time is money, but in reality, time is life. You will continue to lose time because you are losing time!

The difficulty is that if you are excessively frugal with your time, you may become annoying or borderline neurotic. You become intensely irritable. Concentrating on "only doing essential things" becomes monotonous for you and those around you. Even useless things have their purposes in life, which is an apparent contradiction. Sleeping might appear to be a waste of time, but chronic sleep deprivation is more fatal than persistent starvation or thirst.

To become more productive, be mindful of your time management. Observe how you use your energy if you wish to develop intelligence.

Because 90% of human efforts are wasted on trivial activities that have little to no impact on their lives and the lives of those around them, you must be conscious of the activities that sap your strength. When you become energetically compact, however, you begin to discover a treasure trove of previously unknown information. You acquire knowledge from the outside world. It derives from the observations and experiments of others.

In contrast, intelligence is innate, much like intuition or instinct. Your energy sphere has numerous breaches, and this is the problem. And they vary from individual to individual. For others, it is lust/immorality, uncontrollable urges, restlessness, aimless scrolling, low-return activities, and, most commonly, excessive thinking. You will be surprised by how much natural energy is stored in your body once you cease overthinking.

Avoid being hasty with your words and actions. Be conscious of your eating habits and the effects of each meal (consumption, digestion, and assimilation). It is a discipline that permeates your entire life.

There is no need to be inflexible or unbending. You will gain limitless insights and self-awareness if you simply keep a close watch on yourself.

If you have a mental ailment, refrain from complaining.

- You're too afraid to commit your notions to paper.

- I'm too busy to meditate for twenty minutes.

- I'm too indolent to do a 30-minute exercise.

- Unable to slumber for 6 to 8 hours due to disarray

- Your brainwashing prevents you from filtering the information you consume (music, videos, messages, etc.).

Wishful thinking will not lead to success.

Evaluate your options;

What is it that you want?

- What causes you to desire it (is it a fiery desire or a mimetic desire)?

- What are your goals (status, money, independence, or romantic relationships)?

- How will you attain it (what short-term actions will yield long-term results)?

Permit your pupils to perceive changes rapidly.

Permit yourself to be wholly focused on the task at hand.

Permit your hearing to become deafeningly deafeningly deafeningly deafeningly deafen

You dislike going to the gym, but you wish to appear attractive.

You dislike reading but desire an education.

You detest hustling yet want independence.

You dislike socializing but wish to expand your network.

Your willpower must exceed your mind's / body's desire for solace.

Drop, avoid, or minimize the behaviors, attachments, and individuals that prevent you from living your ideal existence.

If you wish to learn how to swim, enter the water.

On desiccated soil, no mental attitude will ever be beneficial.

Chapter 14: Utilize An Effective To-Do List

A to-do list is a list of tasks that must be completed within a specified period of time, such as a day, a week, or even two hours. These lists are helpful because they contain manageable duties, which encourages action and discourages delay.

There are two common methods to organize a to-do list for maximum efficiency: placing the most important items at the top and the less important ones at the bottom, or designing the list so that the tasks progress from the easiest to the most challenging. This enables the creation of reminders and the preservation of order.

The list should be ordered with the most important items at the top and the less important items at the bottom. To-do lists are useful because they consolidate your duties and due dates into a single location.

Your to-do list can include project management tasks, purchasing lists, and even aspirational life changes.

Why Certain To-Do Lists Fail While Others Are Successful

Even if you maintain a to-do list, it is only beneficial if it helps you complete tasks. This is where the distinction between excellent and poor to-do lists becomes apparent.

Extremely Useful Checklist

The following elements comprise an effective inventory of tasks:

Tasks that are attainable, well-described, well-planned, and allow for some flexibility in the event of delays.

Distinguishing between objectives and tasks

As a result, you can complete tasks without feeling overwhelmed. The purpose of a to-do list is to make your tasks appear manageable, as opposed to insurmountable, so that you are less likely to procrastinate due to feeling overburdened.

Inefficient Task List

A poor to-do list, on the other hand, is filled with nebulous tasks that lack clear descriptions and due dates, are awkwardly worded, and fail to differentiate between overarching objectives and more specific sub-objectives.

On a decent to-do list, you would not want to find items such as "get your life in order," "stop sleeping in," and "think of three project ideas immediately." These names provide no encouragement or motivation to act. Use titles such as "Make your bed to improve discipline," "Try sleeping an hour earlier tonight," or "Write down your thoughts on how you can attempt the project" instead.

Chapter 2 We all have 24 hours in a day: Prioritize What Matters

How about establishing 48-Hour Productivity based on a 24-hour day? So many obligations, so little time, correct? Wrong!

Effective time management requires working SMARTER, not harder!

Time management, concentration, and motivation are the foundations for planning, attaining, and becoming more productive. Negatively affecting our productivity, distraction transforms apparently busy days into time wasted.

There never seems to be enough time in the day. But if everyone has the same 24 hours per day, why do some people accomplish more than others?

The solution consists of working wiser, not harder.

The most successful individuals have exceptional time management skills.

You only need to learn the most effective time management and goal setting strategies to prioritize actions that lead to the achievement of your short- and long-term goals in order to live a fulfilling existence.

Being occupied is not synonymous with being effective.

The objective is to accomplish more in less time.

How? Plan your objectives and prioritize your tasks in order to maximize results, reduce tension, and enhance other aspects of your life.

Conclusion

Time management is life management and an essential entrepreneurial talent. This is an essential resource. Time management is the process of finding methods to work smarter, not harder, in order to complete tasks in less time. Time management can be acquired and must be regularly practiced like any other skill. By learning how to manage your time, you grant yourself the ability to be successful and live a life of your choosing. Due to the number of actions required to develop the skills and the time required to conquer them, it can be difficult to gain control of your time. You will be able to accomplish everything you set out to do with less effort and in less time if you use the techniques and strategies outlined in this book to gain control of your time.

If you can exercise fundamental time management techniques for an extended period of time, your productivity will increase dramatically. Previously unattainable objectives will become more attainable. Previously intimidating duties will no longer appear daunting. Things you never imagined possible will begin to occur if you simply show up and put in the effort.

Time is the next best form of currency, so it is crucial that you utilize it wisely. Learn how to effectively manage your time and you will begin to spend more time doing the activities you enjoy.

www.ingramcontent.com/pod-product-compliance
Lightning Source LLC
Chambersburg PA
CBHW050029130526
44590CB00042B/2337